SOLAR COOKING

A Primer/Cookbook

by Harriet Kofalk

Book Publishing
Company

Summertown, Tennessee

Previous edition published as Sol Food by Peace Place Press,
Eugene, Oregon

Kofalk, Harriet, 1937—
    Solar Cooking / by Harriet Kofalk.
          p.   cm.
    Includes bibliographical references and index.
    ISBN 1-57067-007-2
    1. Solar Cookery.   2. Solar ovens.   I. Title.
TX835.5.K64   1995
641.5'8–dc20

Published by **Book Publishing Company**
PO Box 99 - 156 Drake Lane
Summertown, TN 38483

Proceeds from this book support the activities of
Peace Place, a center for inner-peace related gatherings to share
the conscious use of our inner resources.

Table of Contents

DEDICATION
To the Sun of Knowledge,
from whom we learn to use light and might in our own lives.

ACKNOWLEDGMENTS

The Thanks Be To Grandmother Winifred Foundation has supported the completion of this book in its present form. This is their way to honor the needs of older women who want to help women worldwide lead more effective lives. Thanks be to Rachel Winifred Upjohn Light, whose legacy lives on through us all.

Several of the recipes in this book have been adapted for solar cooking from *The Peaceful Cook*, also by Harriet Kofalk. The author is grateful to the many unnamed cooks— and eaters— who have shared their enthusiasm and their recipes herein.

A special thanks to the solar enthusiast authors who gener-ously agreed to have their material republished in this book, to mentor/solar cooker expert Mary Lou Krause, to those who continue to share the experiments in weekly vegetarian cooking classes (also called "The Peaceful Cook"), to Chris Roth who first turned on the solar-cooking light at Peace Place, and to all of you as readers— enjoy!

Let the sun of happiness
constantly remain risen in your heart.

Introduction

Was it just two years ago that I discovered solar cooking? My, how time flies when you're having fun! And solar cooking is fun. That's why it became a passion so quickly: it helps the environment, it's free, and it's fun.

Soon I found myself at the first international solar cooking conference (See "Solar Cooking—It's Free, Fun, and Ecologically Healthful," page 79.) I've used my solar cooker every bright day since, and in the process evolved this book to help others learn about solar cooking, using the most natural, direct energy in one of the most basic acts we all perform each day.

Solar cooking is one of the best and easiest ways that we (particularly women) can help to heal the Earth. Virtually the world over, women are the cooks, and therefore traditionally also the essential firewood gatherers, for in most places the two tasks are inextricably woven together. At the Earth Summit in Brazil, more than 90% of the 17,000 people who passed the solar cooking demonstration exhibit did not know that you can cook without fire. Solar cooking is also a survival skill and tool that is valuable for each of us to know.

No doubt humans have used the sun to cook for a very long time, but two elder women in Arizona have helped us to rediscover the ease of doing it now by creating a do-it-yourself solar box cooker that you can make at home. All you need is two cardboard boxes, some aluminum foil, glue, a sheet of glass, and 3-4 hours of time. A commercial version of their cooker is available through Solar Cookers International; see page 8 for details.

The idea is simple, the benefits many. The most important to our health is the gentleness with which food cooks on any bright day. This creates a whole new perception of food preparation and connection with the Earth that improves health directly as well as on very subtle levels.

Does solar cooking take a lot of time? No, you simply put food in the solar cooker in the morning and take it out—hot and ready to eat—at dinnertime. As if that weren't enough, in tightly-covered pots nothing burns or dries out. It just waits for you to come home to eat. This is true on any bright day, regardless of air temperature. On cloudy days, simply use your stove; this is appropriate technology, not a replacement for the stove. Yet it teaches us that there are choices and there are ways to heal ourselves and our planet through paying attention to both when and how we prepare food.

Many people look for health answers in eating different kinds of food; however, they continue to race through food preparation while doing three other things and listening to distressing news at the same time. It's no wonder our health is affected! When we keep the food preparation area special, devoted to the loving process of creating nurturing food—whether in the kitchen or in a solar cooker—a different dynamic takes place. When we create meals in the sunshine, from the sun, we carry the food preparation process into another dimension altogether.

Energy savings is another significant benefit. Solar cooking needs no special recipes, just a willingness to experiment and to enjoy new ways of creating health. In countries where firewood is increasingly difficult to find and a necessity for most traditional ways of cooking, solar cooking makes even more sense. This country is a model (for better or worse) for many others. By solar cooking food for ourselves, we can also show others its advantages and help on a broader scale than we may have thought possible.

Solar cookers come in many forms. A sampling of economically priced cookers is shown on pages 8-10. Instructions are also included for making a solar box cooker that can easily be constructed at home in a few hours with familiar materials.

In fact, making a simple solar cooker can be done and can be taught using locally available materials anywhere in the world. Using a solar cooker is the biggest challenge, for it represents a fundamental shift in the way we do something every day, often several times a day. Solar cookers can be used on any bright day, regardless of air temperature, thus enriching our lives with a new consciousness about food and its preparation—and our connection with the Earth that nourishes us.

At the conference on solar cooking, when I was very new at this, I asked people their favorite hint for beginners. Without exception, the reply was, "Just do it." That confused me at the time, when it seemed there must be lots of details to learn. Now I understand better that it really is that simple. Solar cooking provides a health benefit that can't be measured, but can certainly be felt—and shared. Just do it. And enjoy!

Harriet Kofalk

Choices
in Solar
Cookers

Life sets priorities that may not include time to make your own solar cooker. If this is your feeling, ready-made commercial alternatives are available. Solar Cookers International (SCI), the tax-exempt organization that promotes the use of solar cookers worldwide, markets a simple solar box cooker. It's portable, folds flat (its outer dimensions are 23" x 27" x 9"), and sells for $58 plus 20% for shipping and handing in the U.S. plus 8% tax for California orders ($30 to ship overseas by surface, $60 by air). This is the cooker illustrated on the front cover of this book.

SCI Solar Box Cooker

SCI is also developing the CooKit, a pre-cut cardboard solar panel cooker, which is being used experimentally in refugee camps and will soon be available for sale. (See the article on pages 85-87 that describes this new form of simple solar cooker.)

SCI also carries other tools of the trade, including plans on how to make and use a solar cooker, available in Spanish and French as well as English. A teaching model, an actual-size paper pattern, and slides and videos for teaching purposes are also available.

SCI CooKit (solar panel cooker)

Another simple cooker available commercially is the Sunspot™. The lightweight stove comes folded as a box, and once unfolded, the four rectangular box-lid reflectors deflect the sun's rays into the center of the box to cook the food. The closed box measures 10" x 10" x 4½". On a clear day, individual portions of various foods can cook at temperatures above 350°F. The cooker retails for $31.95; you can order it by calling Scott Resources (ask for Customer Service), 800-289-9299, or by writing Scott Resources, P.O. Box 2121, Fort Collins, CO 80522.

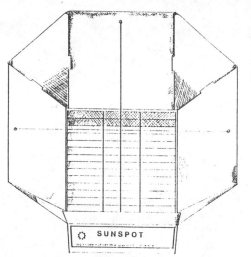

A variety of high-tech, parabolic, and other design cookers can also be found. Real Goods, a company specializing in alternative energy products, carries several, including the Sun Oven, with a fiberglass case and tempered glass door. Because of its design, it reaches temperatures up to 400°F, which is higher than the typical cardboard box cooker.

Choice Connections

Solar Cookers International (SCI), 1724 Eleventh Street, Sacramento, CA 95814; tel. 916-444-6616, fax 916-447-8689

Scott Resources, P.O. Box 2121, Fort Collins, CO 80522; tel.800-289-9299

Real Goods, 966 Mazzoni Street, Ukiah CA 95482-3471; tel. 800-762-7325, fax 707-468-9486

Books and organizations listed on page 92 can guide you to other cookers and solar cooking products.

Making Your Own Solar Cooker

Given the choice, making your own solar cooker is highly recommended, for it's one more way to become more intimately involved with the food you prepare and know exactly how it's cooked. You can easily create your own solar cooker using inexpensive materials. Here's what you'll need:

List of Supplies

1. Two cardboard boxes: The smaller one (your inner box) should be close to the desired cooking area size and depth, at least 18" x 18" x 8" (need not be square). The inner box does not need flaps. The larger one (your outer box) should be 1½"-3" bigger on each side than the smaller box and at least 20" high, including the flaps. (For example, if the inner box is 18" x 18", the outer box should be approximately 21" x 21" x 20".)

Note: Bigger isn't better. It's better to make two smaller cookers (18"-24" on a side) than one bigger one, for better solar efficiency in cooking more than one dish at a time. A box smaller than 18" on a side can be used to warm foods up to 150°F (the restaurant industry standard for hot foods), but does not allow enough movement of heat around the pot for adequate cooking, which requires reaching more than the boiling point (212°F).

2. Pocket knife or small utility (razor blade) knife to cut cardboard

3. Pencils, including one without a point (or a tracing wheel from a sewing store) to score cardboard for bending

4. Yardstick or other linear measuring device

5. 8 oz. of nontoxic yellow wood glue, thinned to 2 parts to 1 of water, or homemade flour-and-water paste

6. Empty container to hold glue, and foam-rubber (or other small) paintbrush to apply it

7. 50-75 feet of aluminum foil

8. Newspaper (avoid pages with colored ink) for insulation between boxes

9. Extra sheet of *firm* cardboard for the reflector, the size of the top of your outer box (21"x 21" for the example above)

10. Aluminum flashing (or other thin metal plate, like a cookie sheet) the size of the bottom of your inner box, to line the bottom

11. Flat, black, *nontoxic* poster paint and brush to paint the metal plate

12. Sheet of clear, clean window glass, at least the size of your outer box (21"x 21" for the example above). An old window in an aluminum frame is easy to handle. If the glass is unframed, edge it in tape for safe handling. There's a trade-off between using single- or double-strength glass. The sun enters more easily through single, but stays in better with double.

13. Approximately ¼ yard of white felt or wool (optional)

14. Oven thermometer (optional)

15. 3 yards of self-stick plastic paper, used for shelf linings (optional)

How to Make a Simple Box Cooker

1. Cut the inner box so the sides are 8" high all around. Glue the bottom flaps of the inner box into place if they aren't already; weight down to hold until glue dries.

Glue down the bottom flaps of the outer box the same way, and weight down to dry.

2. Line the inside of the bottom of the inner box with aluminum foil; glue into place by putting the glue on the box, and lay in the foil, dull side down, on the glue. (Fig. 1) Run the foil up the sides an inch or so to assure good sealing; make sure the foil fits tightly into edges and corners. Cover the outside of the inner box with aluminum foil for extra insulation, glued with shiny side

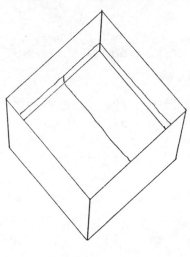

Fig. 1

toward the glue in order to obtain the best reflection of sunlight and make a heat barrier. Patch foil as needed for complete coverage to minimize air leaks.

3. Cut four of the pieces left over from the top of inner box a little smaller than the size of the sides of the inner box; cover the pieces with aluminum foil (glue dull side of foil toward the cardboard). (Fig. 2) Glue these pieces to the inner sides of the inner box for extra insulation.

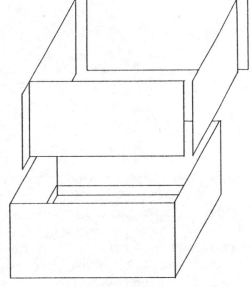

Fig. 2

4. Cut three or four strips of cardboard 2" x 10". Cut a slit ½" in from each end, as shown in Fig. 3. Position these in the bottom of the outer box so that they will steady the inner box when it is placed on top of them. That way, wherever you set your cooking pots inside the inner box, they will be supported by these tripods.

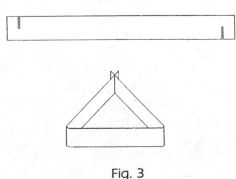

Fig. 3

5. Crumple half-sheets of newspaper into loose balls, and stuff them lightly into the bottom of the outer box around the tripods, but not on top of them.

6. Put the inner box in place inside the outer box. Stuff the space between the sides of the boxes with more crushed newspaper, tightly but not bulging. (Fig. 4)

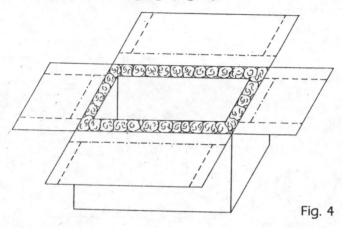

Fig. 4

7. Fold one flap of a long side of the outer box onto the nearest side of the inner box. Score (but do not cut) along the underside of this flap where it meets the edge of the inner box. (Score with a dull pencil or a tracing wheel, being careful and accurate as this process produces the vital flat surface where your glass will rest.) Cut in from each edge of the flap up to the score line just a little deeper than the sides of the inner box, so the resulting flap will fold down loosely into the inner box. (Fig. 5) Repeat this step with the opposite long side. With the remaining short sides, cut in from the edge of the flaps a little deeper than the sides of the inner box, but past the score line all the way to the edge of the outer box.

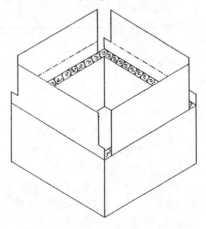

Fig. 5

8. Glue the dull side of foil all around the flaps on the outer box, keeping foil especially smooth on the side that will show inside the inner box.

9. Fold the flaps down into place, and glue if necessary to hold them in place.

Your box is now finished! All that remains is to create the reflector and black metal liner:

1. Score (but do not cut; use tracing wheel if possible) 1½" from one edge of the reflector piece of firm cardboard (Fig. 6). Glue dull side of foil as smoothly as possible to one side of the reflector, up to the score line.

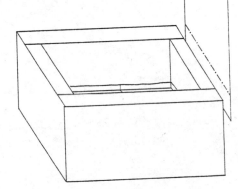

Fig. 6

2. Bend on score line and glue the reflector to the top of the outer box, flush with one long edge of the box, foil side facing the inner box. Weight down to hold until glue dries. (Note: You may use mylar or foiled cardboard instead of foil—whatever you can get that is smoothest and thus most reflective.)

3. Cut the metal liner to the size you want. Paint with flat, black, nontoxic paint; set aside. When dry, lay plate in the bottom of the inner box carefully, so you don't tear the aluminum foil. (If you do tear the foil, patch it well to avoid air leaks.)

4. Cut pieces of felt to glue along the top edges of the box, to provide a smooth, firm resting place for the glass and to seal in the heat. Use extra thicknesses if necessary in places to make the top edge as level as possible and avoid air leaks between the glass and the cooker.

5. Put the glass on top of the cooker. Set the cooker facing the sun with the reflector at an angle (supported by a rock or brick) so the bright spot of sunlight is *within* the box.

An oven thermometer helps you to see how it's doing; it will go to at least 200°F within an hour in bright light, and soon go higher.

6. Put in your food, relax, and wait for dinnertime!

Optional finishing touch : Apply self-stick plastic shelf paper to the outside of the box and to the back side of the reflector to give extra protection from sudden showers and create a finished look to your cooker. Or you can draw designs or messages on the outside. It's your chance to be creative with the original piece of art that you've now completed.

Solar cooker in winter use at Peace Place— at the
edge of the covered porch in case of sudden showers,
facing south where the low angle of the sun can still
reach it fully. In summer, the cooker is placed out in the
middle of the garden. A stand with wheels (like an old TV
stand) helps a lot.

Congratulations! All that's left is to use your cooker— and to
share what you learn with others and with me, please. Experiment, have fun, enjoy!

Using Your Solar Cooker

Now that you have your solar cooker, it's time to use it— the real test of your willingness to create more fun in your life.

Simply place your cooker outdoors on the next bright morning. Aim it so the reflector faces the sun. Raise the reflector to an angle that brings the brightest line of reflected sunlight into the box, and prop the reflector to stay in that position.

Place your food, in a covered, dark pot, inside the box. Put an oven thermometer inside where you can watch it without removing the glass. Place the glass on top.

Stand back and let the sun cook your meal. Enjoy!

Solar cooking requires no special recipes. The following pages contain the most important information you'll need to use your solar cooker; the upper corners of the pages have been tipped in ink so you can refer to them more easily.

Basic Tips for Solar Cooking

To get the most out of your cooker, take a little time to experiment with it. Put it out on every bright day and watch what its temperature does. Learn how (and how often) to adjust the reflector best to maintain the highest temperature and where in your garden or patio it works best. This may change with the season as the sun's angle changes. In my garden, for instance, a large tree casts a morning shadow at certain seasons, but not at others when the sun rises above it rather than through it. Its foliage also makes a difference in how much shadow is cast.

You will soon discover that specific recipes are less important than these tips. Once you understand the principles, you will see how easily you can adapt many of your own favorite recipes to solar cooking. The recipes in this book will get you started so you can more readily understand the principles involved. Enjoy!

1. Store your cooker outdoors (with waterproof cover to protect it from overnight condensation). You'll be more apt to use it more often if it's in position and ready to cook.

2. Raise your cooker's reflector first thing every morning (unless it's raining), so the cooker will begin to warm up. You'll be surprised at how many things you will think of for it to do—and its energy is free! Clear sunshine, not heat, is what you need. You can cook in midwinter on a clear day.

3. Pre-heat your cooker. If it's hot when you put the food in, the food will cook more quickly.

4. Differentiate between cooking and baking. Cooking is simply heating something to meld the flavors, and any time on a clear day works. If you have raw dough (bread, cookies, cake), plan to bake it when the sun is brightest and at its highest angle (usually between 11am and 2 pm, but varies with the season). In the Pacific Northwest, I cook on every bright day year-round, but bake only in the summer months when the sun is at a high angle overhead more of the day.

5. Use dark pots with tight-fitting dark lids because dark colors absorb more heat. I like cast iron because it holds the heat longer, especially with intermittent clouds. Many prefer dark blue enamelware. Corning's smoked-glass Visionware™ also works well, and you can watch how things are cooking without opening the lid of the cooker. Clear glass is OK when baking dark foods (without a

lid, or when topped with a dark lid). You can also wrap a dark towel (or other cloth) around a light-colored pan. Avoid stainless steel, which does not conduct heat well, and aluminum, which many believe is unhealthful.

6. Fill pots only half full or less. Heat then penetrates better and more evenly. For the same reason, cut foods in small pieces to cook better. For baking, cakes less than an inch thick will bake better, as will small cookies.

7. Put a tripod of some sort in the bottom of the cooker, so the hot air can circulate under your pan as well as around it. Raise flat pans (like cookie sheets) with several other pans so the cooking area is as close as possible to the top glass. Most of the heat comes from the top in a solar cooker (unlike an oven, where the heat comes from the bottom).

8. To shorten the cooking time, bring liquid to a boil on the stove first. Put the lid on so it gets hot too (and the food boils faster). The hotter the better, and the faster it will start to absorb solar heat. This is especially helpful in winter months in areas where the sun is available fewer hours or at a low angle. You can finish cooking on the stove if food isn't solar-cooked as much as you want it by mealtime (especially in winter when the sun is at a low angle). Note: This creates a very sticky pan— and the trade-off of using more hot water and human energy to clean it.

9. Most foods cook in approximately twice the time it takes on a stove. But you can simply put food on in the morning, and it will be cooked, hot, and ready to eat by night. If covered with a tight, dark lid, most food will not burn nor dry out, nor will it overcook. When in doubt, you can always cook it longer.

10. Take your time. Solar cooking helps us to remember a more natural sense of time. The sun determines the timing, not the cook. When the sun is high at midday in midsummer, cooking takes the least time. Solar cooking in other seasons works well, and teaches us patience.

11. Keep an oven thermometer in the back inside corner of your cooker. It gives you a gauge of how the cooker is doing and how fast it heats, especially as the seasons change and different timing becomes appropriate.

12. No oil is needed to cook most foods, so you can replace oil with other liquid in recipes, or leave it out (not in baking, however, where oil may be needed to achieve certain textures).

13. Fresh fruits and vegetables need no liquid added for

cooking in covered pots. Grains and beans may need ¼ less liquid than for stove top cooking; experiment to determine the appropriate amount to suit your personal taste. Very little moisture evaporates during solar cooking.

14. Soak beans and grains overnight to shorten cooking time. Even better, instead of just soaking overnight, sprout them. Simply soak them overnight two or three days ahead of time. Then pour off the water (save it for watering plants; it's very nutritious), and rinse beans/grains 2-3 times a day until "tails" of roots sprout. (In hot weather, this often takes only a day; rinse often so they don't spoil.) Refrigerate until ready to cook.

15. Remove the pot lid (or open the glass) as little as possible. Opening the cooker can quickly lower the temperature by 50°F—and more the longer it's open. Plan ahead. Foods don't need stirring because they don't stick or dry out.

16. Always use pot holders. Pans and lids get hot, and we're not used to needing help to pick up a pan sitting outdoors in a box.

17. Wear a visor and sunglasses when working around your solar cooker to protect yourself from getting too much sun or ultraviolet radiation. The reflected light is hard on your eyes, and you're in the sun more than you realize.

18. Glass jars painted on the outside with nontoxic black poster paint work well for cooking small quantities. (Leave a vertical strip unpainted if you want to watch the cooking.)

19. Keep a dark cookie sheet in the bottom for a drip pan and to provide extra heat absorption at the bottom of your cooker. Anything dark in the bottom helps to draw the heat down.

20. Expect the unexpected. Textures are firmer, even when food is thoroughly cooked.

21. With a solar box cooker that has one reflector, angle the reflector so the lightest spot of reflection is over your cooking pot. If you're at home, reposition the cooker to track the sun every couple of hours. If you'll be gone for the day, position the cooker toward the midday sun— and use it to cook, not bake (or be flexible about the results).

22. Just do it! Changing a habit as basic as cooking on a stove requires enthusiasm. Just do it— and enjoy a whole new dimension to your food and your life. Then share your own tips with others, including me.

Preface to the Recipes

To start you on your cooking journey, the remainder of the book contains recipes I've tried and others have also enjoyed. Because I am a vegetarian, all recipes are without meat, fish, or eggs. Although I do not cook entirely vegan meals myself, all the recipes in this book are without any animal products to honor those who choose that way of life. The main difference from my own choice of foods is a shift from sweetening with honey to using maple or rice syrup. To me it's a trade-off (one of many in our lives these days) between supporting a local farmer who lovingly raises her bees organically and does not process her honey, or paying to transport from elsewhere a processed syrup that is not animal-based. Whatever your choice, make it consciously.

Many of the following recipes call for Bragg Liquid Aminos, an unfermented soy product available in natural food stores. It replaces soy sauce, tamari, salt, and similar ingredients with a more healthful balance of amino acids that adds a subtle flavor to recipes.

Cooking for me is one of life's pleasures and one of the best ways I know to keep the subtle energies of life at work on our behalf. Therefore, I choose to grow organically most of my own produce and herbs. When I do buy, I choose to purchase from local organic sources (directly, whenever possible). This also ensures that I buy foods in season. This supports local growers and markets, and provides the most healthful foods to nurture our bodies— and our souls.

For these same reasons, I choose primarily to cook one-dish meals and desserts, my personal favorite way to eat. To give you some ideas, I've selected basic recipes and then provided some variations to show how easily you can exercise your own options of herbs and ingredients. You will soon find how easy it is to adapt almost any recipe to preparation in your solar cooker.

Recipe Table of Contents

(cont.)

Main Dishes and Vegetables

Quiche with a Twist

Walnut Sun Crust, pg. 61
6 cups (packed) chopped fresh kale
2 cups tofu, crumbled
2 Tbs nutritional yeast (optional)
Juice of one lemon
2 Tbs Bragg Liquid Aminos
¼ tsp nutmeg

Prepare Walnut Sun Crust and bake, if possible, a day ahead of time (or in the morning). Be sure to oil the pan before pressing in crust, so it won't stick at serving time.

Lightly steam kale for 5 minutes on the stove. Meanwhile, in a blender, combine other ingredients until smooth, adding 2-4 Tbs of kale cooking liquid if necessary. Keep mixture as thick as possible. Put kale into pie shell. Pour tofu mixture over it. Bake in solar cooker until firm (at least 2 hours, usually).

Serves 6.

Option: You could increase this recipe by one-half: Press crust into the bottom of a 9" x 13" baking dish. Using half again as much of other ingredients, layer kale and tofu mixture. Bake until firm.

Sun-stuffed Cabbage

This recipe suggests steaming the cabbage on the stove rather than in the solar cooker, so the leaves will get tender enough to roll them around the filling. If you raise your own cabbage, this is a great way to use the beautiful, large outer leaves below where it heads, before the head forms and they become too tough.

1 medium cabbage
3 cups crumbled tofu
1 cup cooked brown rice
1 green pepper, chopped
1 Tbs Bragg Liquid Aminos
½ cup raisins
½ tsp paprika
Dash of pepper
3 cups tomato puree

Steam 8-12 large cabbage leaves until tender (may take 45 minutes). If you use a regular head, core and steam head until slightly tender (10-15 minutes). Peel off 8-12 leaves.

Mix remaining ingredients, setting aside 2 cups of puree for topping. Put ½ cup of the filling in the center of each leaf, folding in the ends and rolling leaf around the filling. Place seam side down, close together in a baking dish. Pour remaining puree on top. Cover with a dark lid, and set in solar cooker as long as you wish, at least 2 hours.

Serves 6-8.

Option: If you have more Swiss chard than cabbage, pick twice the number of large leaves, steam very lightly, and use two leaves together to hold filling. Chard leaves are much more tender and harder to handle, but work well.

Black Bean Sun Patties

1 cup black beans
½ cup quinoa, rinsed
½ tsp chili powder
½ tsp cumin powder
1 green pepper, diced
½ cup whole wheat bread crumbs
1 Tbs Bragg Liquid Aminos
Optional garnishes, including shredded soy cheese, soy yogurt, diced avocado, chopped black olives, fresh chopped tomatoes and tomatillos, shredded greens

Soak black beans overnight. Drain, rinse, and add 5 cups of vegetable stock (or fresh water). Add quinoa, cover with a dark lid, and cook in solar cooker all day.

At mealtime, mash cooked beans and quinoa. Add other ingredients, except garnishes. Form into patties and sauté in a skillet with a small amount of oil until lightly browned; turn and brown the other side. Serve with garnishes as desired.

Serves 6 (2 patties each).

Options: This recipe is good served with a side dish of brown rice. The rice can also be cooked in the solar cooker, with dried tomatoes and tomatillos added (or fresh, depending on the season), plus herbs like oregano, as desired.

Sun-stuffed Peppers

When peppers are plentiful at the end of summer, this is a good choice for an autumn dinner. Cooking the rice in vegetable stock (also made in your solar cooker) instead of water not only improves the nutritional value, but adds subtle flavor to the stuffing as well.

4 large green peppers
1 Tbs vegetable oil
½ cup Swiss chard stems, diced (or celery)
½ cup chopped walnuts
2 carrots, grated
2 cups cooked brown rice
½ cup regular or fat-free soy cheese
1 Tbs Bragg Liquid Aminos

Cut a thin slice from the top of each pepper. Scoop out seeds and core. Chop the tops and sauté in oil in a skillet with the chard stems, walnuts, and carrot. Mix in rice, half the soy cheese, and Bragg's. Use this mixture to stuff the peppers. Top with remaining soy cheese. Set them in a dark cooking pot. Cover tightly and set in solar cooker all day.

Serves 4.

Options: Fresh mushrooms can be chopped into the mixture as a good addition. Lentils cooked with the rice add a subtle flavor that enhances all the ingredients.

Chili in the Sun

1 cup dry garbanzo beans
1 cup dry pinto beans
4 cups vegetable stock or water
2 Tbs vegetable oil
2 medium zucchini, chopped
2 large sweet peppers (red or green), chopped
4-5 cups fresh tomatoes, chopped
½ cup tomatillos, chopped (optional)
½ cup chopped fresh parsley
1 Tbs chili powder
1 Tbs each dried basil and oregano
1 Tbs ground cumin
2 tsp fresh ground black pepper
1 tsp fennel seeds
½ cup fresh dill weed or 1 tsp dried dill
2 Tbs fresh lemon juice
2 Tbs Bragg Liquid Aminos

Ahead of time: Sprout beans by soaking overnight, then draining off liquid and rinsing the beans 2-3 times a day for 2-3 days. Put in Dutch oven with vegetable stock, cover with heavy lid, and bring to a boil on the stove (to hasten cooking on shorter solar days). Place in solar cooker and leave all day. This step is best done a day or more ahead of time; the beans can be stored in the refrigerator until ready to fix chili.

On chili-eating day: If solar conditions prevail, omit oil and combine remaining ingredients (except dill, lemon juice, and Bragg's) in the Dutch oven. Place in solar cooker and leave all day. Two hours before eating, add beans— with or without the liquid, depending on your preference— to heat them with the other ingredients.

If solar conditions do not prevail, heat oil in a large skillet on the stove. Add chopped zucchini and peppers, and cook 5 minutes or until slightly soft. Add tomatoes and herbs (except dill, lemon juice, and Bragg's); cook uncovered for 30 minutes, stirring often. Add beans and other ingredients; cook 15 minutes longer.

Serves 6-8.

Autumn in the Sun

2 lbs fresh potatoes
2 lb fresh tomatoes, sliced
1 Tbs fresh basil, chopped fine
2 Tbs Bragg Liquid Aminos
Pepper to taste (optional)
½ lb mozzarella-style soy cheese, sliced
1-2 cups crumbled tofu
1 cup chopped fresh parsley

There are two ways to prepare this dish, depending on whether you expect two successive days of good solar cooking weather.

All-Solar Method: This generally takes two days of good sunlight. Put potatoes in a heavy, dark pan; cover and cook all day in the solar cooker. When cool, cut into thick slices. Complete recipe the next day.

Solar/Top-of-Stove Method: This can be done on one day, but uses a "regular" stove for part of the process. Steam the potatoes on the stove until barely tender. Drain and cut into thick slices.

To complete for either method: In a large, dark baking pan, layer potatoes, 1 Tbs Bragg's, tomatoes, basil, 1 more Tbs Bragg's, pepper (if used), and slices of soy cheese.

Mix tofu and parsley (and pepper if you wish), and spread on top. Top with more soy cheese if desired. Cover with a dark lid, and put in solar cooker for 2-3 hours or longer, enough to melt cheese and blend flavors.

Serves 6-8.

Sun Sweet and Rhubarb

1 cup lentils (red preferred)
2 cups vegetable stock or water
1 large sweet potato, sliced
1 cup rhubarb, diced
2 Tbs maple syrup
1 Tbs curry powder
1 tsp fresh ginger, grated
½ tsp chili powder
¼ cup shredded coconut (optional)

Mix all ingredients, except coconut, in a dark pan. Top with coconut, if desired, and cover with a dark lid. Bake in solar cooker all day.

Options: You may add more stock and serve as a soup. Serve with brown rice for a hearty meal. Chutneys go well with it too.*

Serves 4-6.

*An easy chutney to serve with this, especially when your apple tree is dropping fresh fruit, is to blend together 2-3 tart apples (2 cups) with 1 Tbs lemon juice (to keep apples from turning dark) and ¼ cup raisins. Serve cold or at room temperature. Apples also serve as a digestive aid, so are good to serve with a spicy meal.

Harriet's Impasta

So much of our life we take for granted that we often overlook alternative ways of doing, or thinking, that may give us new insights into who we are. I'd never thought of shredding cabbage to serve as pasta, but here it is. I'd never thought of writing this book about how I like to cook and eat, but here it is.

For impasta:
8 cups thinly sliced cabbage

For sauce:
2 Tbs olive oil (or use ½ sesame oil)
6 cups fresh vegetables, cut in bite-size pieces; may include carrots, broccoli, zucchini, tomatoes, mushrooms, green beans, or whatever else is current in your garden
1 tsp each basil, thyme, oregano—all preferably fresh
¼ tsp ground cloves
½ cup sunflower seeds (optional)
2 lb canned tomatoes (preferably organic) or fresh ones if available
1 Tbs maple syrup
1 Tbs Bragg Liquid Aminos

Place shredded cabbage in a heavy, dark pan. Cover and let it steam (you need add no water; it creates its own liquid) at least an hour (on a very bright day) or two, or longer if you prefer.

To prepare the sauce, either mix other ingredients together and pour them over the cabbage to cook all together, or on top of your stove, sauté vegetables briefly in oil. Add herbs, spices, seeds (if using), syrup, and Bragg's. Simmer until tender, about 5 minutes. Serve over cabbage.

Serves 6-8.

Option: Either serve with a rich dessert, like tofu pudding, or add crumbled tofu or tempeh to the sauce for a complete meal.

Solar Stew

1 Tbs vegetable oil
2 cups brown rice
1 green pepper, chopped
2 Tbs sesame seeds
1 cup white beans
2 cups tomatillos (or fresh chopped tomatoes or puree)
3 cups vegetable stock or water
1 cup corn kernels (or other in-season vegetable)
1 Tbs fresh chopped basil
2 Tbs fresh chopped parsley
½ tsp thyme
1 Tbs Bragg Liquid Aminos

Heat oil in Dutch oven, and sauté brown rice, green pepper, and sesame seeds 3-4 minutes until they begin to brown. Add other ingredients, except Bragg's; cover and set in solar cooker all day. Just before serving, add Bragg's.

Serves 6-8.

Options: Sprout the beans 2 or 3 days ahead of time; soak them overnight, then rinse 2-3 times a day. They'll sprout little tails of roots. At this time, you gain their life force and decrease the cooking time.

Sun Lasagne

½ lb (8 noodles) spinach or whole wheat lasagne noodles
4 cups crushed tomatoes
1 Tbs dried basil or 2 Tbs fresh basil
1 Tbs dried oregano or 2 Tbs fresh oregano
3 cups Swiss chard or other fresh greens, chopped
¼ cup grated soy cheese (Monterey Jack type)
1 lb tofu, mashed
½ tsp nutmeg
1 Tbs Bragg Liquid Aminos
¼ lb mozzarella-type soy cheese, shredded

In a cast iron pot, mix tomatoes and herbs; add chopped greens and cook briefly until they go limp. Remove from pot.

In a separate bowl, mash tofu and mix with grated Jack-style soy cheese. Layer one-third of the tomato mixture, then one-third of the uncooked noodles, and then one-third of tofu mixture, repeating the layers two more times. Top with shredded mozzarella-style soy cheese. Cover tightly and sun-bake half a day or until done.

Serves 4-6.

Note: Lasagne noodles (and other pasta) may not hold up well in this process. The result is still delicious. Enjoy it for what it is, but don't expect it to be like the oven-baked variety.

Tofu with Nuts

1 Tbs vegetable oil
2 cups fresh mushrooms, sliced
½ cup slivered almonds
2 cups vegetable stock or water
1 lb tofu
2 Tbs water
2 Tbs Bragg Liquid Aminos
2 Tbs nut butter, or part tahini (sesame butter)
2 cups whole wheat noodles
½ cup fresh parsley, chopped

In a cast-iron casserole, sauté mushrooms and almonds in oil for 10 minutes, stirring occasionally. Add 2 cups of vegetable stock; heat thoroughly. Meanwhile, squeeze liquid from fresh tofu as much as possible, crumbling it in the process. Mix 2 Tbs water, Bragg's, and nut butter together, and pour over tofu, stirring gently until well mixed.

When mushroom sauce is well heated, top with dry noodles, then pour tofu mixture on top. Cover and bake in solar cooker 3-4 hours, or longer if you wish. Add fresh parsley just before serving.

Serves 4.

Soybean Enchilada Casserole

1 cup soybeans
3 cups vegetable stock or water
4 tomatoes or 1 (28 oz) can organic crushed tomatoes
1 cup fresh oregano leaves (or as much dried as creates an
**   irresistible aroma)**
1 tsp cumin powder (or more)
12 corn tortillas
1 green or red pepper, chopped
1 cup grated soy cheese

Two days before serving this dish, soak soybeans overnight in water. Drain and use the water on your plants; they love its nutrients! Add vegetable stock to beans, and heat in cast iron cooking pot until boiling. Place in preheated solar cooker, and leave it all day. (Note: Soybeans do not get soft when cooked.) Drain off some liquid, if necessary, and cool down. Blend soybeans, a portion at a time, until well ground (need not be smooth).

On serving day, heat tomatoes and herbs in cast iron cooking pot until boiling. Pour into another pan, except for a small amount in the bottom. Layer 3 tortillas, ground soybeans, green pepper, and soy cheese. Repeat for three more layers, including tomatoes, topping last layer with soy cheese. Put in preheated solar cooker until soy cheese on top bubbles (1-2 hours, or all day if you want to meld the flavors more).

Serves 6.

Sunny Couscous

Mints are somewhat interchangeable, depending on your taste preferences. I used peppermint in this, but spearmint or others would work as well. Leftover couscous is great in salad, especially with sprouted rye berries, grated carrots, sliced mushrooms, and other ingredients as you choose, such as edible pea pods; dress with oil and vinegar.

2 cups whole wheat couscous
2 Tbs vegetable oil
½ cup fresh mint leaves
2 cups vegetable stock or water

Heat oil in cast-iron Dutch oven; add couscous and stir until it starts to brown, about 5 minutes. Puree mint leaves and vegetable stock in blender; add to Dutch oven and heat mixture to boiling. Cover and place in solar cooker for the day. Fluffs up and cooks to perfection!

Serves 8.

Pasta Solar Salad

2 cups hot vegetable stock or water
2 cups vegetable pasta
1 Tbs vegetable oil, plus ¼ cup for dressing
4 cups mixed chopped fresh garden vegetables
2 Tbs rice vinegar
2 Tbs fresh basil (or herbs to taste)

Heat stock in a preheated solar cooker (or allow extra time). Meanwhile, pour 1 Tbs oil over the dry pasta. Add to hot liquid. Cover and solar cook 45 minutes. All liquid will be absorbed into the pasta, rather than poured off and wasted. Put pasta in a covered container in the refrigerator to chill until serving time.*

Shortly before serving time, chop fresh vegetables to suit your taste, approximately the same amount as the amount of cooked pasta. (Again, you can vary this to suit your taste. Some like a little salad with their pasta; others like a little pasta with their salad.) Combine vegetables and chilled pasta.

Mix oil and vinegar and herbs, and pour over salad just before serving to 6-8 fortunate people.

*If time allows, save energy by allowing the pasta to cool to room temperature before refrigerating it, so your refrigerator doesn't have to work so hard. Remember that foods lose nutritive value when cut, so save the chopping of vegetables until just before serving time.

Zucchini Sun Feast

2 cups sliced zucchini (or other summer squash)
1 cup sliced tomatoes
1 Tbs fresh basil
1 cup shredded soy cheese

Alternate squash and tomatoes in a dark skillet. Top with basil and soy cheese. Cover and bake as long as you like.

Serves 4.

Option: A cup of brown rice may be put in the bottom of the skillet first, to create a heftier main dish. Add ½ cup vegetable stock or water (the squash and tomatoes create the rest of the liquid needed).

Sunnyside Up Tofu

Great hot or cold, as is for finger food, with a salad or steamed vegetables, in sandwiches, or cut up into a salad. Good road food too— easy to eat and to carry in a small cooler.

1 lb tofu, cut into ½" slices
2 Tbs Bragg Liquid Aminos
1 Tbs grated fresh ginger (optional)

Put tofu in dark skillet. Sprinkle with Bragg's, plus ginger and other herbs as you choose. Cover and cook in solar cooker as long as you wish, from 2 hours to all day. It's "done" any time, just time to meld the flavors. The longer it cooks, the firmer it will be.

Serves 4-6.

Golden Curry

2 cups brown rice
4 cups vegetable stock or water
2 lb tofu, cubed
2 Tbs grated fresh ginger
3 apples, sliced
½ tsp ground cloves
1 tsp cinnamon
½ tsp pepper
1 tsp cumin
1 tsp coriander (optional)
½ tsp turmeric
½ tsp paprika
½ cup raisins
½ cup raw cashews

Bring stock to a boil; add rice. Cover and cook in solar cooker until done — 2 hours or all day. Extra liquid may remain; that's OK, for it will sauce the curry.

Meanwhile, combine other ingredients in a large skillet. Cover and cook in solar cooker until mealtime.

Depending on your eaters, either combine the rice and curry, or serve separately.

Serves 6-8.

Un-cream Sunny Soup

1 cup millet
2½ cups vegetable stock or water
3 Tbs tahini (sesame butter)
1-inch piece of fresh ginger, cut in small pieces
2 cups broccoli leaves and flowers, cut in small pieces
4-6 cups vegetable stock or water
2 Tbs miso (soybean paste) or Bragg Liquid Aminos

Put millet and 2½ cups stock in covered dark pot, and cook in a preheated solar cooker 2 hours or until it absorbs all the liquid. (This can be done a day ahead.) In a blender, put cooked millet, tahini, and ginger. Blend until smooth. In a dark cooking pot, combine millet mixture, broccoli, and remaining stock. Cook 2 hours, or longer. Just before serving time, melt miso in a small amount of the soup, and stir into the whole. Makes a creamed soup that is dairy-free and delicious!

Serves 4.

Black and White Sun Soup

1 cup black beans
1 cup small white beans
6-8 cups vegetable stock or water
2 cups Swiss chard with stems, chopped (or celery)
1 cup diced carrot
1 Tbs cumin seed (or ground cumin)
½ tsp celery or fennel seeds
1 tsp basil
½ tsp chili powder or ⅛ tsp cayenne pepper (optional)
Juice of 1 lemon
2 Tbs Bragg Liquid Aminos

Soak beans together overnight in water; then drain (save water for your plants; it's highly nutritional). To enhance the life force and nutritional value, sprout the beans for two days, if possible, before fixing soup. (See page 34 for directions.)

To cook beans, place them in a heavy pot; add stock and other ingredients (except Bragg's). Cover and heat to boiling. Place pot in solar cooker all day, or as long as possible. Just before serving, add Bragg's.

Serves 6.

Golden Glow Soup

**4 cups cooked winter squash, peeled and cut in small
pieces (carrots or pumpkin also work well)**
4 cups soy milk
**1 tsp *each* ground dry mustard, turmeric, ground ginger,
cumin**
½ tsp cinnamon
Dash of cayenne pepper (optional)
1 cup vegetable stock or water
1 Tbs honey

In a blender, pour 1 cup soy milk and add 1 cup squash; blend
until smooth. Repeat with the remaining squash and milk. Combine all ingredients, cover, and simmer all day in the sun.

Serve hot to 6-8, depending on what else you serve with it.

To cook squash: If solar energy permits on the day before making soup, cut the squash in pieces, put into a deep baking dish,
cover, and steam (no water needed) all day, or until soft. If it's
cloudy or you want to warm the house on a cold day, cut the
squash in half, remove seeds, and place cut side down on baking
pan. Bake at 350°F until soft when you touch it, approximately 1
hour (more or less, depending on size of squash). You can also
bake it whole, which takes approximately twice as long.

Sunbean Soup

8 cups vegetable stock
¾ cup lentil or bean flour
2 Tbs Bragg Liquid Aminos

Dumplings (optional):
   2 cups whole wheat flour
   1 tsp baking soda
   2 Tbs soy yogurt
   2 Tbs vegetable oil
   ¾ cup soy milk or vegetable stock
   ¼ cup chopped fresh parsley
   2 Tbs chopped fresh basil (or other herbs to suit tastes)

Soup stock may be prepared ahead of time or the morning of soup day. (Use only organic vegetables grown without chemicals to avoid creating an unhealthful chemical concentrate.) To prepare stock, fill a dark Dutch oven half-full with stems and inedible portions of vegetables. Cover with water and bring to a boil on the stove (to shorten solar cooking time, unless it's a long midsummer day). Put in the solar cooker to simmer 2 hours or longer. Drain off stock and return to cooker.

Without dumplings: One-half hour before mealtime, remove stock from cooker and add lentil flour, whisking until smooth. At this point, chopped fresh greens may also be added. Return to cooker until mealtime.

With dumplings: Add lentil flour to stock one hour before mealtime. To make dumplings, combine dry ingredients; add wet ones and stir lightly. Drop in spoonfuls on top of the hot lentil soup. Return to cooker until mealtime.

Serves 8.

Desserts

Spring Sunshine Cookies

½ cup molasses
2 Tbs vegetable oil
1 cup grated carrots
2 cups whole wheat flour (may include ½ cup soy flour)
2 Tbs nutritional yeast (optional)
½ tsp cinnamon
½ tsp nutmeg
1 cup nuts, chopped (may include part sunflower seeds)
1 cup date pieces, pitted and chopped
½ cup fruit juice (approx.)

Combine molasses, oil, and carrots. Add dry ingredients and stir. Keep batter as thick as possible, but if it is too thick, add fruit juice to desired consistency. Drop by small spoonfuls on an oiled, dark cookie sheet. Bake in solar cooker until firm, approximately an hour.

Makes 4 dozen.

Open Sesame Cookies

Cumin is a digestive aid, but we rarely associate it with cookies. Sometimes spelled "cominos," its distinctive flavor complements sesame well.

⅓ cup maple syrup
½ cup vegetable oil
¼ cup soy yogurt
1 cup sesame seeds
1 tsp cumin seeds, crushed
rind of 1 orange, grated
1½ cups whole wheat flour

Blend syrup and oil; add soy yogurt and stir thoroughly. Mix in sesame seeds, cumin seeds, and orange rind; then add flour. Drop by small spoonfuls on a dark cookie sheet. Bake in the solar cooker for one hour or until lightly browned.

Makes 3-4 dozen.

Zucchini Sunseed Cookies

Another way to use summer zucchini! And no one will even know it's there, unless you tell them.

½ cup vegetable oil
½ cup maple syrup
2 Tbs soy yogurt
1 tsp vanilla
grated rind of one orange or lemon
2 cups grated zucchini
3½ cups whole wheat flour
1 tsp baking soda
3 cups oats
½ cup combination of slivered almonds (or other locally produced nuts) and sunflower seeds
1 cup carob chips
½ cup shredded coconut
¼ cup fresh peppermint, finely chopped, or ½ tsp extract (optional)

Mix together wet ingredients with a wire whisk. Grate orange rind and zucchini into the bowl. Add dry ingredients and mint, if used. Mix well. Spread half of mixture in a 9" x 13" baking dish for bar cookies. Drop rest of dough by small spoonfuls on an oiled, dark baking sheet. Bake 1-2 hours, depending on cooker temperature (250°F works well), until browned.

Makes 4 dozen.

Oatmeal Raisun Cookies

Learned the hard way!— don't leave the cookies out all day, especially not until the pan cools. When they're done, take them off the cookie sheet, or they stick.

⅓ cup maple syrup
½ cup vegetable oil
2 Tbs soy yogurt
1 tsp vanilla
1 cup whole wheat flour
1½ cups oats
½ tsp baking soda
½ tsp baking powder
1 tsp grated orange rind (optional)
½ cup raisins
¼ cup nuts (optional)

Mix together wet ingredients with a wire whisk. Add dry ingredients, orange rind, raisins, and nuts, and stir lightly, just until mixed. Drop cookies on a oiled, dark cookie sheet. Bake until light brown, approximately one hour at midday.

Makes 3-4 dozen.

Sun-browned Brownies

If the chocolate bug bites you, try this way to appease it (more like fudge than cake).

½ cup vegetable oil
⅓ cup maple syrup
½ cup soy yogurt
1½ cups whole wheat flour
½ cup carob powder or cocoa
½ cup nuts

Mix together wet ingredients with a wire whisk. Add dry ingredients and stir lightly. Pour into a well-oiled 8" x 8" baking pan,* and bake an hour (if you want them soon and the day is very bright) or all day.

Serves 6-8 (or fewer).

*Paying attention to the color of food that's to be cooked in a solar cooker helps us choose appropriate pans. Since the brownies themselves are dark, a glass pan works well for this recipe.

Sunlit Apple Soufflé
(eggless, of course)

1 cup chopped unpeeled apple
1-2 cups crumbled whole-grain bread
¼ cup raisins
1 cup fruit juice or soy milk
½ tsp cinnamon
¼ tsp nutmeg or cardamom
1 Tbs maple syrup
1 Tbs molasses
1 tsp vanilla
1 cup tofu, crumbled
peel of one unsprayed orange (optional)

Layer apples, then bread, in a dark, 9" x 9" baking pan (round cake pan or skillet works well). Sprinkle raisins on top. In a blender, combine other ingredients, and blend until smooth. (Adding tofu last makes it easier to blend). Pour evenly over bread and apples. Cover with a dark lid (a cookie sheet works well), and bake 4 hours (or all day) in the solar cooker.

Serves 4-6.

Apple Sunslump

This recipe is a variation on the one in Louisa May Alcott's famous book, *Little Women*. I've modified it several times over the years, and now once again. Originally it had a cup of sugar. Depending on the sweetness of your apples— and your taste— it can be made without any sweetener.

> 6 cups sliced apples
> ¼ cup apple juice
> 2 Tbs maple syrup (or to taste)
> 1 tsp cinnamon
> ½ tsp nutmeg
> 1½ cups whole wheat pastry flour
> 1½ tsp baking powder
> 2 Tbs vegetable oil
> ¾ cup soy milk or apple juice
> ½ cup raisins

Put apples in a large, dark skillet or baking pan. Combine juice with syrup, cinnamon, and nutmeg, and pour over apples. Cover tightly and cook in solar cooker until an hour before mealtime.

Meanwhile, in a bowl, mix the flour and baking powder well. Gently mix in oil and milk; add raisins and mix until blended. Spoon on top of simmered apple mixture. Cover and simmer an hour (or more) or until dumplings are done.

Serves 6.

Cake

Zucchini is always a challenge to summer gardeners. Slipping it into this moist cake enhances the flavor and the gardener/cook's reputation for innovation.

1 cup whole wheat flour
¼ cup wheat germ
¼ cup carob powder (or cocoa powder)
½ tsp baking soda
1 tsp cinnamon
⅓ cup vegetable oil
¼ cup maple syrup
1 tsp vanilla
2 tsp grated lemon peel
1 cup grated zucchini
¼ cup fruit juice (or soy milk)
½ cup sunflower seeds or nuts
½ cup raisins

Stir together dry ingredients. Add the remaining ingredients and mix gently. Turn into a dark 8" or 9" cake pan; cover with a dark lid, and bake 2 hours in solar cooker, or until edges pull away from the pan.

Serves 6-8.

Golden Cake

This is a good recipe to experiment with, for it's very basic and can be delicious whatever variation you choose.

⅓ cup maple syrup
½ cup vegetable oil
2 Tbs soy yogurt
1 lemon, pulp and finely chopped rind
1½ cups whole wheat flour
2 Tbs sesame seeds
½ tsp baking soda
¼ cup raisins
½ tsp lemon extract

Mix syrup, oil, and soy yogurt with a wire whip until smooth. Add lemon, then remaining ingredients; stir lightly. Pour into oiled, dark pan (10" skillet works well). Cover and bake 2 hours, or until cake pulls away from the sides of the pan or starts to split on top. Long baking won't hurt this one.

Options: Many variations are possible both in flavoring and in fruits. You can replace lemon with 3-4 apples, sliced, or with 1 cup carrot pulp; replace sesame seeds with walnuts and add 2 tsp cinnamon, ½ tsp nutmeg, and increase baking soda to 1 tsp. Or use less syrup for a breakfast cake that's not so sweet. Or fresh pineapple and walnuts for a pineapple right-side-up cake. Pears, berries, or other fresh seasonal fruit also works well. Try mixing a few and enjoy that variation too. Or, . . .

Janie Appleseed Suncake

For the applesauce, windfall apples work great. Simply cut out the bruises or "visiting creatures," and cut into chunks. Put into your solar cooker until soft. Puree in a food mill; or, if you core the apples before cooking, you can puree the apples in the blender, skins and all. You can also simply blend the raw apples and use that for sauce.

½ cup vegetable oil
⅓ cup maple syrup
3 Tbs molasses
1½ cups applesauce
2 cups whole wheat pastry flour
1 tsp cinnamon
½ tsp nutmeg
¼ tsp ground cloves
2 tsp baking soda
1 cup raisins
1 cup coarsely chopped walnuts (or part sunflower seeds)

Mix together the wet ingredients in a large bowl. Add dry ingredients and mix thoroughly. Pour batter into an oiled, 9" x 9" dark baking pan. (The pan can be larger for a thinner cake that bakes more quickly.) Bake 1-2 hours or until a toothpick inserted in the center comes out clean.

Serves 8.

Sun-crisped Apples

6 apples
¾ cup whole wheat flour (or rolled oats ground in a blender)
¼ cup vegetable oil
2 Tbsp maple syrup
¼ cup raisins
½ tsp cinnamon
¼ tsp cloves
½ cup nuts (optional)
1 cup rolled oats
½ cup coconut
1 Tbs fresh lemon juice
Soy yogurt, optional (for topping)

Slice apples thinly or cut in small chunks, and fill a 9" x 13" baking dish half full. Combine flour and oil in a bowl, using a pastry blender or fork until crumbly. Add other ingredients, stirring until well mixed. Spread on top of apples, cover, and bake in solar cooker until apples are tender. Then remove cover to crisp a bit for an hour or so if desired. Good with a dollop of soy yogurt on top.

Serves 6-8.

Option: For a simpler apple suncrisp, simply pour syrup on the apples, and crumble over them a topping of: 1 cup oats, ½ cup whole wheat flour, 1 tsp cinnamon, and ½ cup vegetable oil.

Elegant Cherry Pie

3-4 cups pitted pie cherries
¼ cup maple syrup (or more to suit taste)
1 Tbs agar agar (or cornstarch, mixed with 2 Tbs cold
**   water)**
Sun Flower Crust (see below)

Mix cherries and syrup together in a cast-iron pan. Cover and cook in solar cooker all day. Add thickener and stir until smooth. (If using cornstarch, simmer on the stove until liquid is thick and clear.) Pour into prepared crust; cool until serving time.

Serves 8.

Sun Flower Crust

Sunflower seeds are not only nutritious, they are easy to use and a quick way to create a crust for whatever filling suits the day. They're extremely high in protein, which makes them a most desirable snack as well.

2 cups sunflower seeds
1 Tbs maple syrup
1 Tbs vegetable oil
½ tsp almond flavoring

Blend sunflower seeds in blender until smooth. Add remaining ingredients plus a small amount of water, if necessary, to congeal crust. Press into oiled pie pan. Bake in solar cooker until crust firms, about 2 hours. Cool and fill with cherry filling (or anything else that suits your fancy).

Tofu Sunnyside Up Fruit Pie

Chop fruit just before you plan to use it, as it loses nutritional value when exposed to air. The lemon pulp and juice will help keep apples and peaches from turning dark. And you can enjoy your garden fruits in infinite combinations as the seasons move on.

> **2 cups chopped fresh fruit**
> **2 cups tofu, cut in pieces**
> **⅓ cup maple syrup**
> **½ lemon, peel and pulp**
> **1 tsp lemon extract**
> **Sun Flower Crust**

Using seasonal, local fruits and berries, chop enough to make 2 cups. In a blender, combine tofu, syrup, and lemon peel/pulp/extract until smooth. (Do part of the tofu at a time if your blender objects.) Pour over chopped fruit, and stir gently. Pour into Sun Flower Crust and freeze several hours. Remove from freezer an hour or so before serving to soften slightly.

Serves 6-8.

Options: Red raspberries or strawberries, blueberries, and early green apples like Gravensteins make a colorful combination for a child's birthday party, or 4th of July celebration if that's part of your summer. Keep the combinations of fruits simple so you can enjoy each flavor as they mingle on your tongue.

Strawberry Sun Pie

2 cups fruit juice
2 cups ripe strawberries (or enough to fill a pie crust full)
1½ Tbs agar agar flakes
Walnut Sun Crust (see below)

Bring fruit juice to a boil, then lower to simmer and melt agar agar flakes in it, stirring gently for 5 minutes. Cool 30 minutes. Pour over fresh berries, arranged in a pretty design if you wish. Chill several hours until pie is firm.

Serve plain or with soy yogurt, to 6-8 people.

Options: Instead of fruit juice, crush 1 cup berries in water, and add the grated peel of an orange and 2 Tbs maple syrup.

Walnut Sun Crust

Walnut Sun Crust may be prepared and baked in the late morning and the filling added at noon with plenty of time to bake before dinner time. (Make two crusts while you're at it, and save one for another pie soon.)

1 cup whole wheat pastry flour
¼ cup chopped walnuts
¼ tsp baking powder (optional)
2 tsp cinnamon
2 Tbs maple syrup
3 Tbs vegetable oil

Combine dry ingredients. Add syrup and oil, and mix with a fork until mixture holds together. Press into an oiled 9" deep pie dish. Set in solar cooker for 2 hours (or more if you like it crunchier). Cool until ready to use.

Banana Pie Su(n)preme

2 bananas
⅓ cup maple syrup
1 tsp vanilla
2 cups tofu, in pieces
¼ cup carob chips (optional)
¼ cup coconut (optional)
Walnut Sun Crust

In a blender, combine bananas, syrup, vanilla, and half the tofu. When well mixed, add the remainder of the tofu, and blend until smooth. Put carob chips (if used) into prepared crust. Pour in banana mixture. Top with coconut. Bake until firm (2 hours or more). If the day is bright and the cooking time long enough, coconut will turn golden as well.

Serves 6.

Option: For a simpler variation more like a pudding, you can pour the filling into a dark baking dish, cover, and cook. For a variation in flavor, replace the banana with ½ lemon, cut into pieces. Blend and cook either as a pie or a pudding.

Raisins in the Sun

Walnut Sun Crust, pg. 61
1 cup water
½ lemon, cut in large pieces
2 Tbs cornstarch
¼ tsp nutmeg
½ tsp cinnamon
1 cup fruit juice
2 cups raisins
½ cup plain soy yogurt (optional topping)

Prepare Walnut Sun Crust. While it bakes in the solar cooker (or do it a day ahead of time), prepare filling.

In a blender, combine water and lemon until lemon is chopped fine. Pour into a dark pot; stir in other ingredients until well mixed. Cover with a dark lid, and cook in the solar cooker several hours until it thickens and clears. (If this doesn't happen by mid-afternoon, bring to a boil on the stove, and simmer, stirring, until this happens (only 3-4 minutes). Pour into prepared crust. Cool until serving time. Offer soy yogurt as a topping.

Serves 8.

Slice of Lemon Pie

Lemon is a refreshing flavor any time of year. This takes advantage of the whole fruit in a way that satisfies old tastes in a new way. Finding ways to use the whole fruit is a challenge that's fun. For example, unused portions of the peel (or cores of apples), when organic, can go into the soup-stock pot. They add a fresh flavor to your next batch of stock. If you peel citrus without grating it first, save the pieces of peel in the freezer to grate later when needed. (They grate easily when frozen, another advantage.)

Baked Walnut Sun Crust, pg. 61, or Sun Flower Crust, pg. 59
1 fresh lemon
½ cup fruit juice or water
⅓ cup maple syrup
¼ cup vegetable oil
¾ cup mashed tofu
2 Tbs whole wheat flour

Prepare crust and bake it in the solar cooker. Remove from cooker when the filling is ready.

For the filling, grate the peel of the lemon into a blender. Add juice, syrup, oil, tofu, and flour. Blend until smooth. Peel the lemon and cut the pulp into paper-thin slices. Put slices in the bottom of the pre-baked crust. Pour on tofu mixture. Cover pie pan with a dark lid, and return to solar cooker for the rest of the day.

Serves 8.

Note: If the pie doesn't set (become firm) by mealtime, put it in the oven at 350°F for 15 minutes or until it sets. Cool during dinner. Although it tastes great warm, it's easier to cut when cold.

. . . And
A Few More
(too good
to leave out)

Pickled Sunroots

Sunroots, also known as Jerusalem artichokes or sunchokes, form tubers easily and grow into 8- to 10-foot stalks with bee-attracting yellow blossoms on top. Each year they spread, and you will be hard pressed to dig them all, so you'll always have a good supply. (In fact, be careful where you plant them so they don't take over.) In the fall, simply dig the tubers, scrub well, and eat raw in salads, or cook like potatoes— or make into pickles.

> **2½ cups sunroots, scrubbed and chopped**
> **1 cup green pepper, chopped**
> **1 cup sweet red pepper, chopped**
> **1 cup cider vinegar**
> **1 Tbs dill seeds**
> **2 tsp sea salt**
> **3 Tbs maple syrup**

Mix chopped vegetables in a glass pot. Marinate with vinegar for 15 minutes. Bring to a boil. Add other ingredients and set in a preheated solar cooker for 2 hours or longer. Cool, and then refrigerate.

Makes 1 quart.

Note: If you want to can the pickles, put the boiling ingredients into hot sterilized jars. Put on sealing lids and then set in the cooker until they seal.

Sun Cereal

3 cups rolled oats
½ cup grated unsweetened coconut
½ cup wheat germ
¼ cup oat bran (optional)
¼ cup sesame seeds
½ cup nuts and seeds (walnuts, slivered almonds, pumpkin
  seeds, sunflower seeds—your choice of combinations)
1 tsp cinnamon (optional)
1 tsp vanilla (or other flavoring extract, also optional)

Combine all ingredients in a large, dark baking pan. Mix gently and spread out in a thin layer. Cover (a dark cookie sheet works well); this lid need not fit tightly. Put into solar cooker all day. Store in covered container. I keep mine in the refrigerator to preserve its freshness. Add a handful of raisins just before serving.

Makes 6 cups.

Sunsauce or Fruit Jam

Gleanings of fallen fruit are excellent for this recipe. Simply cut out the bruised or wormy spots, and use the remaining pieces. Nature knows when the fruit is ripest and drops it from the plant or tree. That's when you can pick it up most easily and have the tastiest, sweetest sauce or jam.

Fresh, ripe fruit

Cut fresh fruit into small pieces to fill a heavy, dark pan no more than half full. Cover pan with a tight lid. Cook in solar cooker all day. Makes as much as you want. This is an especially delicious way to make applesauce. You can puree the result in the blender if you prefer a smoother sauce.

For jam, bring the pan in at day's end, and refrigerate overnight. Put the pan in the cooker again the second day. Then it will thicken enough to spread like jam. Add sweetener depending on the ripeness of the fruit and your taste.

Sun Tea

½ -1 cup dried herbs
1 gallon fresh water

In a clear glass jar (gallon size for quantity, or as smaller a size as you wish), put the amount of tea you would use for that amount of water. For a quart— 4 cups of tea— use ¼ cup of herbs, or 3 Tbs. of loose tea (or 3 teabags). For a gallon— 16 cups of tea—you may need less tea per amount of water used, because the tea infuses the water so well in the slow, gentle solar heating. For finely chopped or powdered dry herbs, use ½ cup per gallon of water. Crumble large pieces or whole leaves with your hands. If they're old or you prefer stronger tea, use up to one cup. Experiment. It always tastes good!

Put the tea in the bottom of the jar. Fill with cold water. Screw on the lid. Shake the jar gently to wet the tea; then place it in a sunny place all day. Even in cloudy weather, tea will usually be potable in two days. You can tell by its color (or taste) whether it's strong enough for you. Bring indoors and refrigerate until ready to drink. Keeps well up to a week. Serve hot or cold.

Option: You can also make a single cup (or 2 or more) in your solar cooker. Put the herbs and just enough water for the number of cups you want into a dark container (preferably glass or enameled— without blemish). Cover and put it in your solar cooker all day, and you will have a delicious hot cup of tea waiting for you by mid-afternoon or evening (or sooner).

Note: If using caffeinated tea (black or green tea either alone or as an ingredient in a mixture), strain out the tea leaves before refrigerating. This is not necessary with herb tea, which you can strain when you pour it to drink.

To conserve energy, bring in the jar of tea early in the morning when it's coolest. Then the refrigerator will not have to work so hard to cool it. If you are going to serve it hot for dinner, bring the jar in just before that time. Then the stove will not have to work so hard to heat it.

Sun-baked Crackers

Most of us take for granted that crackers come in a box. We've forgotten how easy they are to make and how delicious they are to eat when you put in your personal favorite flavorings.

1 cup whole wheat flour
1 cup unbleached white flour (or other flour)
2 Tbs wheat germ (optional)
⅓ cup vegetable oil (part sesame oil is good)
1 Tbs Bragg Liquid Aminos
⅓ cup sesame seeds
1 tsp molasses (optional)
Water—a few drops as needed so mixture will stick to-
  gether

Mix all ingredients in a large mixing bowl, adding water as needed until mixture sticks together. Spread dough on a large cookie sheet, and flatten as thinly as possible with a rolling pin. Cut into 1-inch squares (or larger, to suit your taste); leave in place on the pan. Put into the solar cooker, and bake uncovered until they dry sufficiently to feel crisp (takes most of a day, but less when the sun is high). Remove from cooker and from the cookie sheet, and allow to cool. Store in an airtight container.

Makes about 5 dozen.

Options: You can vary the ingredients to suit your pleasure, using different flours, different seeds, sweetened or not. They're delicious with toppings or plain.

Solar Canning and Drying

How to Can in the Solar Cooker

by Eleanor Shimeall
author of *Eleanor's Solar Cookbook*

(In a personal note, Eleanor exclaims, "My canning success has been phenomenal, and if that were the only use for my solar cooker that purpose would be sufficient for my enthusiasm." Need we say more?)

The solar canning method is extremely simple. However, please note this caution! NO VEGETABLES OR MEAT CAN BE CANNED IN THE SOLAR COOKER. Do not even add a sprig of parsley or onion or peppers to tomatoes. There is great danger of botulism in any non-acid food, and it is not possible to detect this.

Use a clean jar (pint, quart, or commercial jar) with a rubber ring inside the lid— thus recycling those odd side jars. No need to sterilize as terminal sterilization occurs while the food is heating in the jar.

Fill the jar with as much fruit as possible without destroying the character of the fruit. Add the amount of dry sugar to your taste (see end of article, next page); then fill jar to neck (not to brim) with water. No need to cook a syrup; sugar and water in the jar will make syrup as the jar contents heat to boiling. Wipe jar edge clean, then place a canning disc on the jar, and screw on the ring tightly. Or screw on the commercial lid with rubber ring inside. No extra force is needed. This is the only time you will tighten the lid.

Fruits and tomatoes need not be peeled. For tomatoes, fill the jar, sometimes adding cherry tomatoes to fill a bit of space, pushing them down until juice is up to jar neck. Leave about ½-inch for heat expansion. Add 1 teaspoon of salt per quart. No water is added as tomatoes make their own juice when packed down.

Jars may be placed in a cold solar cooker, but it will take longer for jars to reach the boiling point. Cooker may be preheated while jars are being filled. One jar takes about one hour. Several may be done at once, but add about ½ hour for additional jars.

Place filled jars on a pie plate or pan to catch any juice that boils out. Watch for bubbling up, and when contents bubble over remove at once from cooker, as juice will continue to boil over and be lost. Use heavy towel or pot holder to lift jars. Let cool on and be lost. Use heavy towel or pot holder to lift jars. Let cool on patio table, covered with a cloth to protect from draft. (No need to add heat to a July kitchen!) Next day rinse the jar, test for seal— a dull thud when you tap the lid. If jars do not seal, add more cooked fruit to fill jar, re-cap, and try again in your solar cooker. Quality is not impaired by two cookings.

This new method is ideal for getting foods into jars at their prime moment— right from the tree or vine into the jar and into the solar cooker in ten minutes. Dark fruits (plums, cherries) and tomatoes heat faster than light (apricots, peaches). Sugar is not necessary for the preserving process. If sugar is not dissolved in sealed jars it will happen in a day or so.

I have also sealed jams, jellies, pickles, chutneys, etc. in the solar cooker when they have failed to seal with open kettle canning.

To sweeten with dry sugar: Sweeter fruits use about ½ cup of sugar per quart. Plums need ¾ cup per quart. Sour cherries 1 cup per quart.

SOLAR-DRYING FOODS

Z DRYER

by Barbara Kerr
author of *The Expanding World of Solar Box Cookers*

A collapsible solar food dryer for use in the back seat of a car, van, old bus, metal shed, garage, empty greenhouse, etc.— any hot, dry enclosure that can be well ventilated.

(In a personal communication, Barbara explains, "The simplest solar food dryer that can handle significant quantities easily is some version of rack and trays such as our Z Dryer. I have made small units for the back of my car and large ones for my backyard where they have occasionally been covered with a sheet or other large cloth to protect from flies or such. I prefer to have the drying food inside a drying cabinet and there are a number of designs available, both updraft and downdraft. In order to keep it simple yet provide protection, a Z Dryer can be placed in any hot, well-ventilated room (attic, screened porch, odor-free garage, spare room, green house, or solarium, etc.). I recently realized that a modern tent with screened ventilators might provide insect and animal control, hot dry air, and eliminate the need to bring trays in at night. In addition, a Z Dryer and tent combination could be folded up during the off-season or carried fairly easily to a source of food.)

Choosing Your Dimensions

Dimensions depend on where the dryer will go. These dryers have been built in varying sizes, from two feet up to five feet high.

Set the tray size first. Larger trays are more convenient, not to exceed about 36" x 24" outside measurement. Be sure the tray *when level* will go through the door of the car or other enclosure you are using. In a vehicle, height should not obscure the driver's rear view. It simplifies if all trays in a household are the same outside measurement.

Materials

Framing: any light wood— 1 x 2, 1 x 1, or strips of plywood
Small nails, non-toxic white glue, open-mesh nylon curtain

material, 12 medium-sized screws, 4 small plastic cups, light cotton drape

Construction of Z-Frames

A. Lay four upright frames (▌) side by side. Draw lines across them every four inches, leaving 6 to 8 inches at the bottom of the frames.

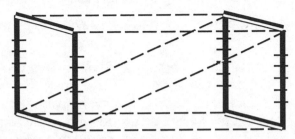

B. Glue and nail support pieces (—) on at the lines.

C. Glue and nail Z-braces on (— —). Sides are identical.

D. Screw cross-braces (▬▬▬) on ends to connect the two Z frames. Do not glue, as these braces are removed to store. Trays should fit with ⅛- to ¼-inch clearance. Big frames may need one more Z, opposite where trays go in.

Construction of Trays

A. To keep uniform outside measurements if using scrap wood of different widths, cut wood for the longest side first. Width of short pieces may vary from tray to tray. Length of short pieces equals outside measurement minus widths of both long pieces.

B. Use butt-ended corners rather than mitered corners; they are simpler and stronger.

C. Glue the frame joints and lay out the tray frame. Work can be done on newspaper, with one side along the column line and the other side along the print line to assure a true right angle.

D. Pulling the joints together, glue and nail on the corner braces. If wood is very thin, flatten the nail point on the other side. Glue is most important to give strength.

E. Lay flat and press with a weight on each corner until dry. Trays can be stacked for drying, with newspaper between.

F. When tray is dry, staple or tack on nylon mesh, turning the edge under into a bed of glue. Leave edge of frame free of fabric so tray will slide smoothly.

Sun Drying in a Nutshell

Selection: Dry only foods still good to eat. May be quite ripe, but not spoiled.

Preparation: Wash hands and equipment before handling food. Wash food well. Cut pieces ⅛- to ¼-inch thick. Small, thin pieces dry fastest. Sizes should be uniform to get even drying. Pre-treatment is rarely needed. Native dryers do not usually blanch or sulfur their food. Fruit may be dipped in an acid fruit juice to help preserve color (lemon, lime, bitter orange, green citrus juice). If desired, fruit may be blanched in scalding water (or without water in a solar oven 160°F to 200°F for 20 minutes) to sterilize. This helps during humid weather.

Spreading: Lay food on tray with space between pieces so air circulates well. After first drying day, the food can be moved closer together progressively as it dries. Beans, apple rings, and other firm foods may be strung on a clean string and hung above the trays.

Drying: Do not expose food to open air, as it may contain pesticide spray, car exhaust, etc. Drying should be done in an enclosure or under a clean cotton drape, at this time in history.

Sunlight will bleach food and destroy some nutrients. Food dried in the dark has better color and nutrition. Food dries by circulation of low-humidity air. It does not need high temperatures; 110°F will do fine. Nutrient loss increases above 120°F.

Check food daily; turn and stir. If any piece starts to mold, pick it out before spores form, and then wash your hands.

Testing: Fruit and tomatoes are dry when leathery. Vegetables should be "rattle dry." Well-dried produce stores best, since insects and mold cannot grow in well-dried food.

Storage: Package dried food in small units in small brown bags. Mark contents and date on the bag in dark pencil (some inks are poison). Place brown bags in small, heavy plastic bags, and seal well with a tie or masking tape. If desired, use a second label outside of plastic bag. Place several small packages in a larger, heavy plastic bag. Then store in a well-closed plastic bucket or other insect-proof container. As the food is used, keep an eye out for miller moths and weevils. If either is seen in the storage container, locate the source and remove it immediately. If widespread infestation threatens, maximum food value may have to be sacrificed by heating dried food in that container to 120°F for 10 minutes. Then store in new bags.

Records: Keeping a drying record is not essential, but useful. Record description of food, type of days when it was dried, location of dryer, and length of drying. Also a record of foods in storage helps in planning for their use.

Use: Dried food may be eaten directly or it may be rinsed with water and set aside to soften. It may be soaked overnight, added to stew without soaking, or may be powdered in a blender to use as soup or seasoning.

Insect control: Do not use insecticides. Put feet of dryer in cups of water if necessary to deter ants. Cover dryer with cotton drape to protect from dust and flies. Fasten drape with clothespins.

Tray care: Trays can be flushed with water and lightly scrubbed if necessary.

A good book is *Dry It, You'll Like It* by Gene MacManiman, POB 546, Fall City WA 98029.

For information about Solar Box Ovens, please write Kerr Enterprises, Inc., POB 576, Taylor AZ 85939.

(reprinted with permission of the author, who is also the original developer—with Sherry Cole—of the most popular solar box cooker design in use today)

Solar Cooking:
More
Perspectives

SOLAR COOKING

It's Free, Fun, and Ecologically Healthful

by Harriet Kofalk

Appropriate technology is basic to the new world view that many of us are embracing. This requires taking advantage of our technological knowledge and using it appropriately, in healing ways rather than destructive ones. Yet one of the oldest, simplest, cleanest, cheapest technologies is still least used: solar energy.

Did you know that you can cook without fire? At the UN conference [on the environment and development, UNCED] in Brazil [summer 1992], more than 90% of the people who passed the booth demonstrating solar cooking did not. Many of them were from countries where wood is scarce, where people— mostly women— spend up to 30% of their time looking for firewood. Over all, more than half the trees cut down in the world are cut to provide wood for cooking. Yet we can *all* cook much of the year without fire, without wood.

Getting this message to peoples of the world is the aim of Solar Cookers International [SCI, 1724 Eleventh Street, Sacramento CA 95814; telephone 916/444-6616], which recently held the first World Conference on Solar Cooking in California. Close to 200 attended, representing five continents and bringing together designers, producers, and users of solar cookers.

The most popular solar cooker is a "box in a box," but a whole range of designs works. The principle involves simply using the sun's energy rather than wood or another nonrenewable source. Typically, a solar box cooker is made from two cardboard boxes, one that fits inside the other. Tightly woven baskets, grass mats, and other materials can also work. The in-between space is stuffed with crushed newspaper or with straw, wool, or other material for insulation. Both boxes are lined with aluminum foil glued to the cardboard. The inner box has a metal plate on the bottom, painted with nontoxic black paint to draw the heat downward. A sheet of glass fashioned in a cardboard frame forms the lid and holds in the heat. One side of the box has another piece of cardboard (also lined with foil) glued to it. It stands up and forms the reflector to send the sun's rays downward through the glass into the box, trapping the sunlight's radiant heat energy. On a clear morning (the temperature is less important than the clarity of sunlight), the temperature inside the cooker can reach 200°F in a half-hour, and stays between 300°-350°F during several hours midday [in seasons when the sun is at its highest angle overhead]. Food is placed in heavy dark pots with lids.

A major advantage of solar cooking is that food can stay in all day without burning, overcooking, drying out, or sticking to the pot. If that's not enough, solar cooking is free! To bake [compared to cooking], you need to turn the cooker hourly or so in order to allow the reflector to track the sun; but for most cooking needs, you can simply put in the food in the morning and take it out at dinnertime, hot and ready to eat. There are other advantages as well: Pots are easy to clean, and— in this country at least— you can finish cooking on the stove if the sun disappears. Instead of storing solar energy, you are storing energy in the cooked food. Fire bricks inside the stove can hold the heat for cloudy periods during the day. Heat-therapy wrap can be heated in one. You can cook first, then heat water for cleaning dishes, also for desalinization and purification. You can dry items like flour and farina with *no* insect infestation in up to three months of storage (in India, where such invasion is usually much quicker).

From around the planet came new numbers: 100,000 solar cookers in use in China; 5,000 in Switzerland; 50,000 sold in India as part of an integrated rural development program; 5,000 distributed in Pakistan; thousands in the Sudan, where solar courses are being started in public schools.

There were stories of other successes, like Senegal, where local carpenters build them, local women train others to use them. At a Montessori school in Arizona, children build solar cookers to heat their lunches. Senior centers in Texas make cookers with help from the University of Texas Energy Center. Refugee camps in Afghanistan, Sudan, and Somalia use them. In Tanzania, straw sleeping mats are cut up to make them, stuffed with dry grass or wood shavings and sewn with a wooden needle. World organizations like Boy Scouts and Girl Scouts are spreading the idea. The Sacramento (California) Municipal Utility District buys them to loan to schools to teach solar cooking. The district has published a solar cookbook and has just released a video on how to construct a "box in a box" solar cooker (available from SCI, which also has a kit available).

As Agnes Klingshirn of the German Agency for Technical Cooperation warned, "Solar cooking doesn't prevent deforestation or desertification and therefore can't solve it, so it should not be billed as such." But it can certainly contribute to a more positive global picture, with benefits such as saving carbon dioxide both directly and indirectly (what the trees *would* have given off if they had not been cut). Cookstoves burning wood produce more than CO_2 because of incomplete combustion.

Shyam Nandwani of India, working in Costa Rica at the National University, noted that we must be honest with disadvantages as well as advantages. Disadvantages mentioned include the fact that its most effective hours are between 9 am and 2 pm [ed. note: that's for baking; you can heat food, even boil water, almost all sunlit hours]. The glass top to the cooker can be difficult to obtain and can break. Heavy-gauge plastic can be used, but its toxicity over a long term is in question. Solar cookers can't meet all the cooking needs of families in some places, such as cooking tortillas for a morning meal, but they can replace a large amount of the wood and other nonrenewable energy sources currently being used, especially in this country.

The challenge is not in making a solar cooker, but in creating something people will *use*. Changing the way we cook is a very basic change to the way we live. At the conference this was termed "cultural inertia." We need a *people*-oriented project, not just one focused on technology. Attitude is a major key to the success of solar cooking. Mohamed El-Bashir of the Islamic Relief Agency in Sudan urged all to consider themselves as "pioneers of peace. This is an *un*harmful device useful for anyone— for *all* living creatures. Solar cooking contributes to global awareness as well as global appropriate technology— free of charge, a unique contribution to the future of [hu]mankind."

Many designs for cookers were described, and some were demonstrated in the Summer Solstice heat wave during the conference. They ranged from a high-tech parabolic model from Switzerland to a low-tech "found materials" model used for the past 12 years by Joe Radabaugh, who lives and cooks from his van. Other models included one of concentric circles of parabolas, variations on solar box cookers including a corrugated plastic prototype, and reflectors of mylar rather than aluminum foil and with four panels instead of one. Some have developed alternatives like a plug-in unit for cloudy days. In order to minimize cultural inertia, some are working on ways to bring the solar power indoors, so cooking can be done there. As Ibrahim Olivi of Saudi Arabia asked, "in hot weather in the tropics, why go outside to cook?"

The field of solar cooking is wide open. As cookbook author Eleanor Shimeall told the assembled group, "Part of getting up every day is to put out the cooker. It's just like a miracle to have that out there— a life-changing style and totally fun!" (She accidentally discovered that you can also easily can fruit in one, even small amounts.)

Keynoter Karim Ahmed, of the Committee for the National Institutes of Environment, reminded us that solar cooking "is a very basic paradigm shift in the way we look at technology [and] really fits in with the Small Is Beautiful movement as part of the larger cultural revolution. The technology must be small and simple, user friendly, empowering, and bring personal fulfillment and joy. A solar box cooker is the best use of the greenhouse effect— after the greenhouse itself." Solar cooking keeps food in a larger context of agricultural technology that's sustainable (as in organically grown food), and of health, recycling, and other technologies that are being developed worldwide.

The quiet revolution has already begun. Small *is* beautiful, and we who appreciate, use, and promote more uses of solar energy are already part of it. As we do our own solar cooking, we can spread the word with the food, and then look back to these beginnings and smile— while enjoying our gently solar-cooked meals.

(excerpted from an article in Talking Leaves, a global journal of spiritual ecology and activism, Lammas 1992)

Solar Cooking Spreads to Fifty Countries

by Solar Cookers International

Solar cooks in at least fifty countries worldwide are using solar cookers to conserve fuel, reduce air pollution, and create a sustainable energy future.

"In our part of the country, wood is hard to find and butane gas costs a great deal," says Norma O., a working mother in the town of Trinidad in northern Honduras. "I am better off than other people because my solar cooker means I don't have to spend precious money buying gas or waste time searching for wood."

Mrs. Sarah D. of Tsensete, Zimbabwe, also says solar cooking offers a distinct advantage over the wood fires which currently cook about one-half of the meals eaten each day on planet Earth. "This is cheaper. There is no pollution— You save wood— Once I started, I never stopped."

"The few people who know of solar box cookers are always happy cooking with them," adds Innocent H. of Ho, Ghana.

Solar cooking is increasingly attractive in many developing countries as an alternative to traditional fuels such as wood and dried animal dung. Shortages of cooking fuel will affect 2.4 billion people by the year 2000, mostly in Africa, Asia, and Latin America, according to United Nations' projections.

Small enclaves of solar cooks are busy perfecting and demonstrating a practical solution in many countries where local fuel shortages are already grim.

In Haiti, for example, the Centre D'Energie Alternative has a network of nearly twenty solar cooks, similar in size to several other small solar cooking groups in Haiti. A group called CIDECI in Chiapas, Mexico, reports 300 users of solar cookers there. Proceso-Tonotiuh, one of several solar cooking groups in Nicaragua, claims 130 families have solar cookers. Scores of villagers in Villa Seca, Chile, have become solar cooks in the past few years, and some have begun making and selling cookers to other villagers.

In Africa, the Sunstove Organization in Crystal Park, South

Africa, reports that over 250 people have become solar cooks. Solar Tech in Shomolu, Nigeria, reports more than 50 solar cookers have been made. Trans World Radio in Nairobi, Kenya, has helped over 200 people become solar cooks. In Mbeya, Tanzania, the Itili Women's Training Centre is training its first group of ten women to be teachers of solar cooking skills.

Solar cooking is also being tried by groups in Argentina, Belize, Costa Rica, the Dominican Republic, Ecuador, El Salvador, Guatemala, Honduras, Panama, Peru, Ethiopia, Indonesia, the Philippines, Sierra Leone, the Gambia, Venezuela, and dozens of other nations.

The governments of both China and India have been promoting solar cooking for more than ten years. Chinese sources indicate that more than 100,000 cookers are in use there. In India, a manufacturer, Surya Jyoti Devices, reports that company alone has produced 500,000 solar cookers.

SERVE, a non-governmental agency in Pakistan, introduced solar box cooking in refugee camps, where thousands of families now cook with the sun.

Hundreds of organizations such as Rotary Clubs, Girl Guides and Girl Scouts, school teachers, Peace Corps volunteers, and women's networks around the world have started programs in the last five years to teach others about solar cooking. Much of the recent surge in solar cooking awareness and activity has been through efforts by a California-based, non-profit organization called Solar Cookers International (SCI).

The popular box cooker that SCI promotes also makes it easy to heat drinking water to temperatures high enough to kill germs. Disease-bearing water is a leading cause of death, particularly among children, worldwide.

For more information, write to SCI, 1724 11th Street, Sacramento CA 95814.

(excerpted from a news release sent by SCI)

THE NEW SOLAR PANEL COOKER

Excitement is rising in the world of solar cooking, since a new design, simpler and more portable than even the solar box cooker, hit the scene recently. First described by Roger Bernard of the Universite de Lyon, France, it was dubbed the Bernard Solar Panel Cooker by *The Solar Box Journal* in February 1994. It was headlined as "a simple, portable model that may open new horizons," and especially appealing for people living or traveling alone, families where a single member has a special diet, elderly people who feel reluctant to carry a heavy box, or teenagers wishing to build and experiment with their own cooker.

You place your food in a black cooking pot and position it on the base of the cooker panel. Then you cover it with a colorless, glass salad bowl (or cooking bag). The bowl shouldn't be wider than the base of the cooker. The side panels of the reflector catch the sun's rays as it travels across the sky, reducing the need for repositioning the cooker during the day.

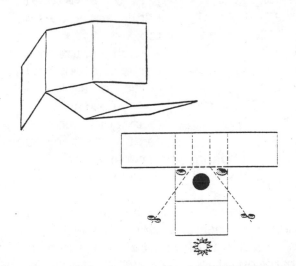

Solar cooking expert Barbara Kerr then tested it and offered some thoughts and her own modifications.

Eye damage is a distinct possibility, so users must be particularly careful to wear protective sunglasses. A nurse by profession, Kerr comments, "By limiting ourselves to flat, foil-covered panels, the danger of eye damage is greatly reduced but remains a problem. Retinal damage, which can occur when sunlight shines into the eyes, is not painful. You cannot tell it is happening, but a retinal burn produces permanent damage and can result in blindness. Be extremely careful if using anything that concentrates the light or reflects the sunlight directly into your eyes."

Her modification included panels that are "all the same size, which then fold to form a flat packet which is so small and light-weight that it can be used by backpackers and others who do not have space for much storage."

Kerr also found an oven cooking bag to be a better cover than a glass bowl. (Plastic bags tend to melt.) "Place the cooking pot in an oven cooking bag with the opening at the top so you can open the bag, check the food, and seal it again without disturbing the cooking. And that part of the bag is usually dry. This is important because food in a panel cooker usually does need to be stirred and checked, since the heat is not as even."

Leona Christie

She experimented with ways to close the oven cooking bag and found neither clothespins nor paper clips satisfactory. A twist tie works well, and needn't be twisted, just wrapped tightly around the bag top.

Some of the finer points mentioned in the articles to date include:

- Glue another rectangular piece of cardboard to the bottom section to better insulate the bottom of the cooking pot

- A few rocks on either side of the wing mirrors help in windy weather

- A more convenient way of keeping the reflective system in good shape is to mount the panels on a wooden board in which you drive a few nails on each side of the wing mirrors to keep them in their correct position.

- It is not necessary to maintain a constant tracking of the sun. A big vertical nail at the front of the board can act as an "orientation indicator." Its shadow should be seen on a white triangular piece of paper glued on the board.

- Allow adequate space at the top of the cooking pot, so it

doesn't boil over. Vigorous boiling means higher cooking temperatures, so "food does not have the delicately enhanced flavor of food cooked in a solar box cooker," according to Barbara.

- A canning ring or other "elevator" helps to keep the cooking pot off the cardboard bottom and allow more air circulation. Dark elevators work best. Barbara muses, "I put three little pebbles, dark and oiled, under a pot. That seems to work even better. I like that— three little pebbles used in memory of the historic three-stone fire that has served humanity for thousands of years. Women, nostalgic for the wood fire where there is no more wood, might even take tiny pieces of wood and form a little 'fire' within the pebbles under the pot. It would keep us from feeling so torn away from roots."

- When cooking at lower latitudes than 45° (Paris, France), the vertical reflectors become less effective. More testing is needed. Roger Bernard is interested to hear results from readers who live in other parts of the world, and Barbara Kerr is interested as well.

Since the first articles were published on solar panel cookers, further modifications have been made. Solar Cookers International has now come out with a Solar CooKit, promoting it as "even far cheaper, tougher, and more transportable" than their box cooker— which Barbara also developed. SCI extended the reflectors to interlock for wind stability and added cooking power, creating a protected "nest" for the pot. They claim "it handily pasteurizes water and cooks up to about 3 pounds of food. It appears to be ideally suited to campers, backpackers, homeless, and large-scale emergency relief efforts."

The SCI Solar CooKit design is made from 2 pieces of bendable, sturdy, shiny material. It also uses a black, covered pot, a coil of rope or other material under the pot to lift it 1-2 cm, and a clear plastic bag to put the pot and coil into.

Barbara Kerr sums up the state of the art, "Solar cooking continues to get simpler. I have put major attention on simple solar cooker designs for 20 years, working to have them easier and more accessible to everyone. Today, I held a Solar Panel Cooker and realized our 20-year mountain of work had truly brought forth a mouse. A mighty mouse! Simplicity is so difficult— difficult to see, not difficult to do, once the idea forms. I think that box-style cookers will remain part of the solar kitchen where time, materials, and circumstances dictate, but the SPC has opened up a new level of simplicity."

Developing an Intuitive Feel for the Dynamics of Solar Box Cooking

by Tom Sponheim

Editor, *Solar Box Journal*

Have you ever wondered why you yourself didn't come up with the idea of the solar box cooker?

Why didn't it occur to us naturally that a double-walled, foiled cardboard box covered with a sheet of glass could easily reach cooking temperatures? I think I know why.

We don't seem to have an intuitive grasp of the properties of insulating materials and the *greenhouse effect*. As we shall see, in the case of insulation properties, we somehow fail to apply our sense of what would keep our body warm to what would keep the food warm inside a solar cooker. I will also propose a way of developing an intuitive understanding of the greenhouse effect.

People newly introduced to solar box cookers find it unfathomable that such high temperatures could be contained in a simple box, perhaps made of only a few layers of cardboard. Obviously the cardboard is able to keep the heat from leaking out. One way to access our intuitive sense for insulation is to imagine that you have to pick up a hot pot handle with your bare hand. That, of course, would be painful. What if you used a piece of paper between your hand and the handle. You would probably get just as burned only an instant later than before. Now imagine using a piece of corrugated cardboard as a pot holder. You could be pretty sure that the heat would never reach your hand with enough intensity to burn you. Next imagine you used two pieces of cardboard, then two pieces separated by a few centimeters of air space. You quickly get a feeling for how much insulating effect such a configuration would provide.

Another helpful device is to imagine putting on a vest or shirt made from various materials. Picture being cold and then donning a vest made out of a sheet metal. You would probably feel even colder. When people ask whether you could make a solar box out of bare bricks, you can ask them how they would feel wearing a vest made out of little brick tiles. Everyone knows that that would not provide much protection from the cold. Our experiences with keeping warm ourselves cause us to gravitate toward soft, light, fluffy substances such as cloth or paper. The food in the oven is like our bodies— what would make us cold would also lower the temperature the food *feels.*

The greenhouse effect isn't much more difficult to understand. While glass has been available for centuries, the idea that you could use it to trap enough heat to actually cook food has occurred rather infrequently. This effect causes the heat from sunlight to accumulate inside any closed space with a glazed opening (e.g., a parked car). Why was this missed for so long? I believe it was because part of the greenhouse process is invisible to our human eyes.

There are two principal kinds of light operating in a solar oven: normal visible light and invisible infrared light. When you look into a solar cooker, the visible light inside doesn't seem to be that much brighter or more concentrated than the sunlight striking us as we stand and look in. Our bodies are certainly not getting hot enough to burn, much less cook, so intuition tells us that food in the oven wouldn't cook either. Our intuition is right as far as it goes. The visible light isn't intense enough to do the cooking, but an invisible transformation is taking place.

When the visible light hits dark-colored objects inside the oven, its energy is absorbed by the object and then re-radiated out in the form of infrared light. We can't see this infrared light, but can we sense it? Sure! Even when you stand many meters back from a large fire on a cold night you feel the warmth of the fire against your face. The fire itself isn't touching you and the air around you is still cold. What you feel on your skin are these invisible infrared rays.

We are left with one last question: What happens to the infrared light? Does it bounce back out of the cooker and back toward the sun? The infrared rays attempt to radiate back out through the glass, but because these rays are fundamentally different from the visible light rays, they cannot penetrate the glass. Instead they are absorbed by the glass, which heats up and radiates some of this energy back inside the oven. This energy then heats the pots even more.

So the picture looks like this: Sunlight (which is actually a mixture of visible light and infrared light rays) streams steadily through the glass into the cooker. When these rays hit the dark pots or black bottom tray, they change into infrared light. This light then becomes trapped inside, bouncing back onto the pots, heating them more, creating more infrared rays which bounce back, etc. This keeps on until the oven reaches amazingly high temperatures.

Why doesn't the cooker keep on heating forever? Well, as the temperature rises, a larger and larger proportion of the heat leaks out through the walls and the glass. The temperature continues to rise until the amount of energy coming in equals the amount going out.

As you can see, it isn't necessarily so complicated. You can use your eyes to see the visible light, your skin to feel the infrared light, and your imagination to see the way the light is transformed and then trapped inside the oven. In this way you develop an intuitive sense for how a solar box cooker works. And we can use our intuitive sense of what would keep our bodies warm to have a sense for what will also keep food warm inside the cooker.

(reprinted from Solar Box Journal #17, June 1994, with permission of the author)

Ancient Light Giver Infuses Food with Energy in a Solar Oven

by Virginia Heather Gurley

The ancient ones around the world have known of the power of the sun. Most modern dwellers are only dimly aware of the sun's vast potential and its intrinsic connection to photosynthesis— the formula for life on planet Earth. We have lost sight of our celestial cosmology where the powerful Light gives organization and definition to human vision.

We can reconnect to the sun as a source of energy and life-giving power by a simple discovery of solar cooking. A full physical manifestation of light occurs in the power of solar cooking. In solar cooking, we tap the power of the sun and fill our personal energy fields with sunlight food. The food is enhanced and blessed by the Central Fire. With a solar oven, we participate in an ecological, spiritual awareness.

We are radiant light— within us. We live by the Sun. Indeed, solar cooking offers a relationship with the environment that is harmonious. The pure and natural solar radiation affects the energetics of the food and endows it with extraordinary bio-nutrition.

Solar cooking is a whole, new, fresh approach to cooked foods. Solar cooking is superior to dry heat methods of conventional gas and electric stoves. Solar cooking also offers an environmental alternative to using firewood for cooking food. It is the vital rays of the sun which cook the food. The essential juices of each vegetable, grain, or meat are retained by the live dynamics of the sun. Solar cooking requires a new definition. "Nutritional physics" is the term given to express the quality of solar cooked, energized food.

The sun (spirit) enters into the earth food (matter) and creates in the broadest sense an alchemical union. When we engage in eating solar infused food, we are participating in this synthesis. The power of the sun becomes a beneficial ingredient in the food itself.

May the Sun of Knowledge, shakti (powerhouse) of life guide us to use solar light in cooking our food.

(Ms. Gurley is a solar cooking specialist. Her cookbook, Solar Cooking Naturally, is available from SunLightWorks, Box 3388, Sedona AZ 86340.)

Postscript and Resources

Many other kinds of solar cookers exist, and more are being invented all the time. The ones I've mentioned are the simplest I know. Please experiment with others as the spirit moves you. Find the one that works best for you in your own life. There are parabolas, indirect (heat panel outside, cooker indoors), and multi-sided variations on the box.

The most popular of the multi-sided solar box cookers is Heaven's Flame. See the book by that title by Joseph Radabaugh. He has been cooking on one solely (and sol-ly!) for 13 years. His book includes a rundown on many other cookers, as well as instructions for making your own Heaven's Flame.

Here are some of the resources I've found helpful in learning about solar cooking:

Gurley, Virginia Heather, *Solar Cooking Naturally,* SunLightWorks, Box 3388, Sedona AZ 86340.

Halacy, Beth, and Dan Halacy, *Cooking with the Sun—How to Build and Use Solar Cookers,* Morning Sun Press, POB 413, Lafayette CA 94549

Home Power—The Hands-on Journal of Home-made Power, POB 130, Hornbrook CA 96044-0130

Kerr, Barbara Prosser, *The Expanding World of Solar Box Cookers,* Kerr-Cole Solar Box Cookers, POB 576, Taylor AZ 85939

Radabaugh, Joseph, *Heaven's Flame—A Guidebook to Solar Cookers,* Home Power Inc., POB 275, Ashland OR 97520

Sacramento Municipal Utility District, *Solar Box Cooking,* POB 15830, Sacramento CA 95852-1830

Shimeall, Eleanor E., *Eleanor's Solar Cookbook,* Cemese Publishers, 7028 Leesburg Place, Stockton CA 95207

Solar Cookers International (SCI), 1724 Eleventh Street, Sacramento CA 95814; telephone 916/444-6616. (SCI also publishes the *International Directory of Solar Cooker Expertise and Advocacy,* first edition, 1994.)

Solar Box Journal, Solar Box Cookers Northwest, 7036 18th Avenue NE, Seattle WA 98115

P.S. As I write this list, I discover that *all* of the books listed have been self-published, as was the one you're reading, originally. This speaks to the joy we who discover solar cooking want to share. Enjoy!

Index

About the Author

Harriet Kofalk lives in Oregon, in an organic garden with a house in the middle called "Peace Place," where she solar cooks all her food, and for guests, every bright day year-round. As part of an Earthstewards Network project called "PeaceTrees" that involved an international group of young adults, she coordinated solar cooking the main daily meal for fifty people for eight days. She teaches vegetarian cooking and leads "plerkshops" ("play + work = all I do," she explains), among them one called "Food for Thought" about the awareness we can bring to food preparation. She also speaks at conferences on agri-spirituality, returning the sacred to the production of food. Previous books include *The Peaceful Cook—More Than a Cookbook* (available from Book Publishing Company, see page 96), poetry, and the biography of a pioneer naturalist.

For those interested in a broader perspective on the recipes in this book, the author invites you to write her with comments and questions at Peace Place, 175 E. 31st, Eugene, OR 97405. A "spiritual supplement" in the form of the self-published earlier editon, titled *Sol Food,* is available for $6.00 postpaid. For each recipe, it contains a short paragraph to focus one's thoughts while preparing the dish, as well as earth-connecting ideas for some of the ingredients, such as a gardening tip; and poetry by the author.

More excellent cookbooks from

Book Publishing Company

Almost No-Fat Cookbook $10.95
Chef Neil's International Vegetarian Cookbook 5.00
Cookin' Healthy with One Foot Out the Door 8.95
Ecological Cooking: Recipes to Save the Planet 10.95
Fabulous Beans 9.95
Foods That Cause You To Lose Weight 12.95
Good Time Eating In Cajun Country 9.95
Holiday Diet Cookbook 9.95
Instead of Chicken, Instead of Turkey 9.95
Judy Brown's Guide to Natural Foods Cooking 10.95
New Farm Vegetarian Cookbook 8.95
Now & Zen Epicure 17.95
Physician's Slimming Guide 5.95
Shoshoni Cookbook 12.95
Simply Heavenly 19.95
The Sprout Garden 8.95
Solar Cooking 8.95
Tofu Cookery 14.95
TVP® Cookbook 6.95
Uncheese Cookbook 11.95
Vegetarian Cooking for People with Diabetes 10.95

Ask your store to carry these books,
or you may order directly from:
The Book Publishing Company
P.O. Box 99
Summertown, TN 38483

Or call: 1-800-695-2241
Please add $2.50 per book
for shipping